MEXICAN All COOKBOOK

Delicious and healthy recipes to fry, roast and bake from all round mexico

Rolando T. Costa

Copyright © by Rolando T. Costa 2024. All rights reserved.
Before this document is duplicated or reproduced in any manner, the publisher's consent must be gained. Therefore, the contents within can neither be stored electronically, transferred, nor kept in a database. Neither in Part nor full can the document be copied, scanned, faxed, or retained without approval from the publisher or creator.

TABLE OF CONTENT

Introduction   **3**

Above Mexican Air Fryer   5

Techniques and Tips for Mexican Air Fryer   6

Air fryer Safety measures for beginners   10

Mexican Pantry   13

Chapter 1: Mexican Air Fryer Appetizer Recipes 18

1. Crispy Avocado Fries with Chipotle Mayo   18

2. Chicken Quesadilla Rolls   19

3. Mexican Street Corn Cups   20

4. Chorizo Stuffed Jalapeños   21

5. Salsa Verde Chicken Taquitos   22

6. Shrimp Tostadas with Avocado Crema   23

7. Crispy Queso Fundido Bites   24

8. Chile Lime Chicken Wings   26

9. Crispy Black Bean Empanadas   26

10. Mexican Street Corn Nachos   27

Chapter 2: Mexican Air Fryer Side Dishes Recipes   **29**

1. Crispy Plantain Chips with Chili Lime Salt   29

2. Mexican Street Corn Salad   30

3. Crispy Mexican Cauliflower Bites   30

4. Spicy Sweet Potato Wedges   31

5. Cilantro Lime Rice   32

6. Cheesy Mexican Street Corn Dip   33

7. Air Fried Guacamole Stuffed Mushrooms   33

8. Chile-Lime Zucchini Chips   34

9. Black Bean and Corn Quesadilla Triangles   35

10. Jicama and Mango Salad Cups   36

Chapter 3: Mexican Air Fryer Main Dishes Recipes 37

1. Crispy Chicken Tacos with Avocado Lime Crema 37
2. Air Fried Beef Tostadas 38
3. Air Fryer Shrimp Tacos 39
4. Crispy Carnitas Burrito Bowls 40
5. Air Fried Fish Tacos with Cilantro Lime Slaw 41
6. Air Fryer Chicken Fajitas 42
7. Chile Relleno Casserole 43
8. Barbacoa Quesadillas 44
9. Air Fried Chicken Enchiladas 45
10. Air Fryer Beef Tamales 46

Chapter 4: Mexican Air Fryer Dessert Recipes 48

1. Churro Bites with Chocolate Dipping Sauce 48
2. Sopapilla Cheesecake 49
3. Mexican Chocolate Lava Cake 50
4. Tres Leches Bread Pudding 51
5. Pineapple Empanadas 52
6. Cajeta Stuffed Churro Twists 53
7. Mexican Flan Cups 54
8. Mexican Hot Chocolate Cookies 55
9. Dulce de Leche Banana Empanadas 56
10. Mango Coconut Rice Pudding 57

Chapter 5: Mexican Air Fryer Quick Fries Recipes 58

1. Crispy Chili Lime Sweet Potato Fries 58
2. Mexican Street Corn Fries 59
3. Spicy Guacamole Fries 61
4. Queso Fundido Loaded Fries 61

5. Adobo Seasoned Crispy Fries — 62
6. Jalapeño Popper Loaded Fries — 63
7. Tajin Lime Zucchini Fries — 64
8. Mole-Inspired Sweet Potato Fries — 66
9. Chili Garlic Avocado Fries — 66
10. Chipotle Ranch Potato Wedges — 67

Conclusion — **69**

Introduction

Welcome to the savory symphony of flavors where the age-old culinary artistry of Mexico meets the modern marvel of air frying. ¡Bienvenidos a "Mexican Air Fryer Recipes Cookbook"! Embark on a gastronomic journey that seamlessly blends tradition with innovation, creating a tapestry of delectable dishes that are as vibrant as they are effortless.

In this culinary odyssey, we invite you to discover the magic of Mexican cuisine reimagined through the lens of the air fryer—a kitchen companion that adds a crispy twist to beloved classics. From the sizzling streets of Mexico City to the heartwarming kitchens of abuelitas, each recipe in this collection encapsulates the essence of Mexican culture while embracing the convenience of contemporary cooking.

Whether you're a seasoned chef or a kitchen novice, our carefully curated recipes promise to transport you to the sun-kissed landscapes of Mexico with every bite. Prepare to tantalize your taste buds with the zest of lime, the kick of chili, and the rich tapestry of spices that define Mexican culinary excellence.

So, don your apron and let the aromas of our Mexican air fryer delights infuse your kitchen. ¡Buen provecho! Get ready to elevate your cooking experience with a touch of Mexican flair and the innovative prowess of the air fryer.

Above Mexican Air Fryer

"Mexican Air Fryer" is a culinary revolution where the time-honored flavors of Mexico meet the innovative efficiency of air frying. This cookbook seamlessly blends traditional Mexican recipes with the modern convenience of air fryers, offering a crispy twist to beloved classics. From street food favorites to home-cooked staples, each dish captures the essence of Mexican cuisine without compromising on health or authenticity. The air fryer transforms cooking, providing a guilt-free and quick alternative to traditional methods. Get ready to embark on a flavorful journey that marries tradition and innovation, bringing the vibrant tastes of Mexico to your kitchen with a satisfying crunch. ¡Buen provecho!

Techniques and Tips for Mexican Air Fryer

Mastering the art of Mexican Air Fryer cuisine involves a blend of traditional techniques and smart tips to ensure your dishes achieve the perfect balance of flavor and crispiness. Here are some techniques and tips to elevate your Mexican Air Fryer creations:

1. Preheat for Perfection: Just like an oven, preheating your air fryer is crucial. Leave it for some minutes to reach the desired temperature before adding your ingredients. This ensures thorough cooking and a crispy finish.

2. Embrace Marination: Marinate your ingredients before air frying to infuse them with authentic Mexican flavors. Allow meats, vegetables, or even tofu to soak up the marinade for at least 30 minutes, enhancing taste and tenderness.

3. Use a Light Oil Mist: While one of the benefits of air frying is reducing oil usage, a light mist of oil can enhance crispiness. Consider using a cooking spray or a brush to apply a oil to your ingredients.

4. Rotate and Shake: Periodically shake or rotate the air fryer basket to ensure even cooking.

This prevents sticking and guarantees that every side of your dish gets that delightful crunch.

5. Layer Wisely: Avoid overcrowding the air fryer basket. Give your ingredients some space to allow hot air to circulate, promoting even cooking and a crisp exterior.

6. Temperature Awareness: Familiarize yourself with recommended cooking temperatures. Higher temperatures are great for a quick crisp, while lower temperatures allow flavors to meld and ingredients to cook through.

7. Parchment Paper Prowess: Use parchment paper to prevent sticking and make clean-up a breeze. Ensure the paper doesn't cover the entire basket, allowing air to circulate.

8. Timing is Key: Keep a close eye on cooking times. Air frying is generally faster than traditional methods, so adjust your cooking times accordingly to avoid overcooking.

9. Experiment with Seasonings: Embrace the rich tapestry of Mexican spices. Experiment with cumin, chili powder, garlic, and lime to add depth and authenticity to your dishes.

10. Get Creative with Toppings: Elevate your air-fried creations with fresh toppings like cilantro, salsa, guacamole, or a squeeze of lime. These add a burst of flavor and a touch of freshness.

Air fryer Safety measures for beginners

Ensuring safety while using a Mexican air fryer is paramount to enjoying the culinary experience without any risks.
Below are some essential safety tips to keep in mind:

1. Read the Manual: Familiarize yourself with the user manual provided by the manufacturer. Each air fryer model may have specific safety instructions and guidelines.

2. Place on a Flat Surface: Always place the air fryer on a stable, flat, and heat-resistant surface. Avoid using it on flammable surfaces or uneven surfaces.

3. Adequate Ventilation: Ensure proper ventilation around the air fryer. Avoid placing it against walls or near other appliances to allow sufficient airflow and prevent overheating.

4. Maintain Clearance: Maintain adequate clearance around the air fryer, keeping it away from curtains, paper towels, or any other combustible materials.

5. Use in a Well-Ventilated Area: If using the air fryer indoors, make sure the area is well-ventilated. The appliance can produce some smoke, especially when cooking certain foods.

6. Keep a Watchful Eye: Do not leave the air fryer unattended while it's in use. Regularly check the progress of your cooking to prevent any mishaps.

7. Avoid Overfilling: Follow the manufacturer's guidelines regarding the maximum capacity of the air fryer. Overloading the basket can impede air circulation and affect cooking performance.

8. Be Mindful of Hot Surfaces: The exterior of the air fryer, particularly the basket and handle, can become hot during operation. Use oven mitts or tongs when handling hot components.

9. Regular Maintenance: Keep your air fryer clean by regularly removing and cleaning the basket and tray. Follow the manufacturer's instructions for maintenance to prevent the build-up of grease and debris.

10. Check for Damaged Parts: Before each use, inspect the air fryer for any damaged parts or frayed cords. If you notice any issues, refrain from using the appliance until it's repaired or replaced.

11. Use Proper Utensils: When preparing or removing food, use utensils that are suitable for air fryers, such as silicone or wooden tools. Metal utensils can damage the non-stick coating.

12. Unplug When Not in Use: After cooking, unplug the air fryer and allow it to cool down before cleaning. This reduces the risk of accidents and prolongs the life of the appliance.

Mexican Pantry

Building a well-stocked pantry for your Mexican air fryer adventures is essential for quick and flavorful cooking. Here's a list of pantry staples that will help you create a variety of delicious and authentic dishes:

1. Cornmeal or Masa Harina: Essential for making crispy coatings for dishes like empanadas or coating vegetables for air frying.

2. All-Purpose Flour: Useful for breading or making dough for certain recipes.

3. Cornstarch: Adds an extra level of crispiness to your air-fried creations.

4. Spices and Herbs:
- Cumin
- Chili powder
- Paprika
- Oregano
- Ground coriander
- Garlic powder
- Onion powder

5. Adobo Seasoning: A versatile seasoning blend used in many Mexican dishes.

6. Dried Chilies: Ancho, guajillo, or chipotle can add depth and smokiness to your recipes.

7. Mexican Chocolate: Ideal for making mole or adding a unique flavor to desserts.

8. Dried Epazote: A traditional Mexican herb that adds a distinct flavor to certain dishes.

9. Rice and Grains:
  - Long-grain rice
  - Quinoa
  - Mexican rice mix

10. Tomatoes:
  - Diced tomatoes
  - Tomato paste
  - Crushed tomatoes

11. Beans:
  - Black beans
  - Pinto beans
  - Refried beans

12. Chilies and Peppers:
  - Diced green chilies
  - Chipotle in adobo
  - Jalapeños

13. Salsas and Hot Sauces:
- Salsa verde
- Red salsa
- Hot sauce (e.g Cholula or Tapatio)

14. Broth or Stock: Chicken or vegetable broth adds depth to various recipes.

15. Pickled Ingredients:
- Pickled jalapeños
- Pickled red onions
- Pickled carrots

16. Vegetable Oil: Suitable for air frying and general cooking.

17. Olive Oil: Extra virgin for drizzling or finishing dishes.

18. Apple Cider Vinegar: Adds acidity to dressings or marinades.

19. Guacamole or Avocado Salsa: Can be used as a topping or dip.

20. Crema: Mexican sour cream adds a creamy element to dishes.

21. Queso Fresco or Cotija Cheese: Crumbly Mexican cheeses for garnishing.

22. Tortillas: Corn and flour tortillas for tacos, quesadillas, or wraps.

23. Lime: Adds a bright citrus flavor to many dishes.

24. Cilantro: Fresh cilantro for garnishing.

Chapter 1: Mexican Air Fryer Appetizer Recipes

1. Crispy Avocado Fries with Chipotle Mayo

Ingredients:
1. 2 ripe avocados, sliced
2. 1 cup breadcrumbs
3. 1 teaspoon cumin
4. 1 teaspoon chili powder
5. Salt and pepper to taste
6. Cooking spray

Instructions:
1. In a bowl, combine breadcrumbs, cumin, chili powder, salt, and pepper.
2. Dip avocado slices into the breadcrumb mixture, ensuring they are evenly coated.
3. Place in the air fryer basket, spray with cooking spray.
4. Air fry at 375°F (190°C) for 8-10 minutes or until golden brown.

Serving: Serve with chipotle mayo for dipping.

Cooking Time: 10 minutes

2. Chicken Quesadilla Rolls

Ingredients:
1. 1 cup cooked shredded chicken
2. 1 cup shredded cheese
3. 4 flour tortillas
4. 1 teaspoon cumin
5. 1 teaspoon garlic powder
6. Salsa for dipping

Instructions:
1. Mix chicken, cheese, cumin, and garlic powder in a bowl.
2. Spoon the mixture onto each tortilla, roll them up.
3. Place in the air fryer basket and air fry at 375°F (190°C) for 6-8 minutes.

Serving: Slice and serve with salsa.

Cooking Time:8 minutes

3. Mexican Street Corn Cups

Ingredients:
1. 4 cups cooked corn kernels
2. 1/2 cup mayonnaise
3. 1/2 cup cotija cheese, crumbled
4. 1 teaspoon chili powder
5. Lime wedges for serving

Instructions:
1. In a bowl, mix corn, mayonnaise, cotija cheese, and chili powder.
2. Spoon the mixture into individual serving cups.
3. Spoon the mixture into individual serving cups.
4. Place the cups in the air fryer basket and air fry at 375°F (190°C) for 5-7 minutes until the edges are golden.

Serving: Squeeze lime wedges over each cup before serving.

Cooking Time: 7 minutes

4. Chorizo Stuffed Jalapeños

Ingredients:

1. 12 jalapeños, halved and seeds removed
2. 1/2 cup cooked chorizo
3. 1 cup cream cheese
4. 1 cup shredded cheddar cheese
5. 1 teaspoon smoked paprika
6. Fresh cilantro for garnish

Instructions:

1. In a bowl, mix cooked chorizo, cream cheese, cheddar cheese, and smoked paprika.
2. Stuff each jalapeño half with the chorizo mixture.
3. Arrange in the air fryer basket and air fry at 375°F (190°C) for 10-12 minutes until the jalapeños are tender and cheese is melted.

Serving: Garnish with fresh cilantro.

Cooking Time: 12 minutes

5. Salsa Verde Chicken Taquitos

Ingredients:
1. 2 cups shredded cooked chicken
2. 1 cup salsa verde
3. 1 cup shredded Monterey Jack cheese
4. 10 small flour tortillas
5. 1 teaspoon ground cumin
6. 1/2 teaspoon garlic powder

Instructions:
1. In a bowl, mix shredded chicken, salsa verde, cheese, cumin, and garlic powder.
2. Spoon the mixture onto each tortilla, roll them up tightly.
3. Place in the air fryer basket and air fry at 375°F (190°C) for 8-10 minutes until golden and crispy.

Serving: Serve with guacamole or sour cream for dipping.

Cooking Time: 10 minutes

6. Shrimp Tostadas with Avocado Crema

Ingredients:
1. 1 pound of medium shrimp, peeled and deveined
2. 1 tablespoon taco seasoning
3. 1 tablespoon olive oil
4. 8 small tostada shells
5. 1 cup shredded lettuce
6. 1 cup diced tomatoes
7. Avocado crema (blend 1 ripe avocado, 1/4 cup sour cream, and lime juice)

Instructions:
1. Toss shrimp with taco seasoning and olive oil.
2. Air fry shrimp at 375°F (190°C) for 5-7 minutes until cooked.
3. Assemble tostadas with shrimp, lettuce, tomatoes, and a drizzle of avocado crema.

Serving: Garnish with cilantro and lime wedges.

Cooking Time: 7 minutes

7. Crispy Queso Fundido Bites

Ingredients:

1. 1 cup shredded Oaxaca or Monterey Jack cheese
2. 1/2 cup chorizo, cooked and crumbled
3. 1/4 cup diced tomatoes
4. 2 tablespoons chopped fresh cilantro
5. 12 small corn tortillas

Instructions:

1. Cut tortillas into small rounds using a cookie cutter.
2. Air fry tortilla rounds at 375°F (190°C) for 3-4 minutes until crispy.
3. Top each round with cheese, chorizo, and tomatoes.
4. Air fry for an additional 2-3 minutes until the cheese is melted.

Serving: Sprinkle with cilantro before serving.

Cooking Time: 4 minutes

8. Chile Lime Chicken Wings

Ingredients:
1. 2 pounds chicken wings
2. 2 tablespoons olive oil
3. 2 tablespoons chili powder
4. 1 teaspoon smoked paprika
5. Zest and juice of 2 limes
6. Salt and pepper to taste

Instructions:
1. Toss chicken wings with olive oil, chili powder, smoked paprika, lime zest, lime juice, salt, and pepper.
2. Air fry at 400°F (200°C) for 25-30 minutes until the wings are crispy and cooked through.

Serving: Serve with additional lime wedges.

Cooking Time: 30 minutes

9. Crispy Black Bean Empanadas

Ingredients:
1. 1 cup black beans, mashed
2. 1/2 cup diced onions
3. 1/2 cup corn kernels

4. 1 teaspoon ground cumin

5. 1 teaspoon chili powder

6. 12 empanada wrappers

Instructions:

1. In a bowl, mix mashed black beans, onions, corn, cumin, and chili powder.

2. Spoon the mixture onto each empanada wrapper, fold, and seal the edges.

3. Air fry at 375°F (190°C) for 10-12 minutes until golden.

Serving: Serve with salsa or guacamole.

Cooking Time: 12 minutes

10. Mexican Street Corn Nachos

Ingredients:

1. 1 bag tortilla chips

2. 2 cups cooked corn kernels

3. 1 cup crumbled cotija cheese

4. 1/2 cup mayonnaise

5. 1 teaspoon chili powder

6. 1/4 cup chopped fresh cilantro

Instructions:

1. Spread tortilla chips on the air fryer basket.

2. Top with corn, cotija cheese, and drizzle with mayonnaise.

3. Air fry at 375°F (190°C) for 5-7 minutes until the cheese is melted.

Serving: Sprinkle it with chili powder and cilantro before serving.

Cooking Time: 7 minutes

Chapter 2: Mexican Air Fryer Side Dishes Recipes

Here are 10 Mexican Air Fryer side dish recipes for you:

1. Crispy Plantain Chips with Chili Lime Salt

Ingredients:
1. 2 ripe plantains, thinly sliced
2. 2 tablespoons olive oil
3. 1 teaspoon chili powder
4. Zest of 1 lime
5. Salt to taste

Instructions:
1. Toss plantain slices with olive oil, chili powder, lime zest, and salt.
2. Air fry at 375°F (190°C) for 8-10 minutes until crispy.

Serving: Sprinkle with additional chili lime salt before serving.

Cooking Time: 10 minutes

2. Mexican Street Corn Salad

Ingredients:
1. 4 cups cooked corn kernels
2. 1/2 cup mayonnaise
3. 1/2 cup crumbled cotija cheese
4. 1/4 cup chopped fresh cilantro
5. 1 teaspoon chili powder
6. 1 clove garlic, minced

Instructions:
1. In a bowl, mix corn, mayonnaise, cotija cheese, cilantro, chili powder, and garlic.
2. Air fry at 375°F (190°C) for 5-7 minutes until warmed through.

Serving: Garnish with additional cotija cheese and cilantro.

Cooking Time: 7 minutes

3. Crispy Mexican Cauliflower Bites

Ingredients:
1. 1 head cauliflower, cut into florets
2. 1 cup breadcrumbs
3. 1 teaspoon ground cumin
4. 1 teaspoon garlic powder

5. 1/2 cup grated Parmesan cheese

6. 2 eggs, beaten

Instructions:

1. Dip cauliflower florets in beaten eggs, then coat with a mixture of breadcrumbs, cumin, garlic powder, and Parmesan.

2. Air fry at 375°F (190°C) for 12-15 minutes until golden and crispy.

Serving: Serve with salsa or a cilantro lime dipping sauce.

Cooking Time: 15 minutes

4. Spicy Sweet Potato Wedges

Ingredients:

1. 2 large sweet potatoes, cut into wedges

2. 2 tablespoons olive oil

3. 1 teaspoon smoked paprika

4. 1/2 teaspoon cayenne pepper

5. Salt and pepper to taste

Instructions:

1. Toss sweet potato wedges with olive oil, smoked paprika, cayenne pepper, salt, and pepper.

2. Air fry at 400°F (200°C) for 15-20 minutes until golden and cooked through.

Serving: Sprinkle with additional smoked paprika before serving.

Cooking Time: 20 minutes

5. Cilantro Lime Rice

Ingredients:

1. 1 cup long-grain white rice
2. 2 cups chicken or vegetable broth
3. Juice of 2 limes
4. 1/4 cup chopped fresh cilantro
5. Salt to taste

Instructions:

1. Cook rice in the broth until done.
2. Fluff rice and toss with lime juice, cilantro, and salt.
3. Air fry at 350°F (175°C) for 5-7 minutes to enhance crispiness.

Serving: Garnish with extra cilantro and lime wedges.

Cooking Time: 7 minutes

6. Cheesy Mexican Street Corn Dip

Ingredients:
1. 2 cups cooked corn kernels
2. 1 cup shredded Monterey Jack cheese
3. 1/2 cup mayonnaise
4. 1/4 cup chopped green onions
5. 1 teaspoon chili powder
6. 1/2 teaspoon cumin

Instructions:
1. In a bowl, combine corn, cheese, mayonnaise, green onions, chili powder, and cumin.
2. Transfer to an oven-safe dish and air fry at 375°F (190°C) for 8-10 minutes until bubbly.

Serving: Top with additional green onions and serve with tortilla chips.

Cooking Time: 10 minutes

7. Air Fried Guacamole Stuffed Mushrooms

Ingredients:
1. 12 large mushrooms, stems removed
2. 2 ripe avocados, mashed

3. 1/2 cup diced tomatoes

4. 1/4 cup diced red onion

5. 1 clove garlic, minced

6. 1 tablespoon lime juice

Instructions:

1. In a bowl, mix mashed avocados, tomatoes, red onion, garlic, and lime juice.

2. Stuffed mushroom caps with the guacamole mixture.

3. Air fry at 375°F (190°C) for 10-12 minutes until mushrooms are tender.

Serving: Garnish with cilantro before serving.

Cooking Time: 12 minutes

8. Chile-Lime Zucchini Chips

Ingredients:

1. 2 large zucchinis, thinly sliced

2. 2 tablespoons olive oil

3. 1 teaspoon chili powder

4. Zest and juice of 1 lime

5. Salt and pepper to taste

Instructions:

1. Toss zucchini slices with olive oil, chili powder, lime zest, lime juice, salt, and pepper.

2. Air fry at 375°F (190°C) for 8-10 minutes until crispy.

Serving: Sprinkle with additional chili powder before serving.

Cooking Time: 10 minutes

9. Black Bean and Corn Quesadilla Triangles

Ingredients:

1. 1 cup black beans, drained and rinsed
2. 1 cup corn kernels
3. 1 cup shredded cheddar cheese
4. 1 teaspoon ground cumin
5. 1/2 teaspoon garlic powder
6. 8 small flour tortillas

Instructions:

1. In a bowl, mix black beans, corn, cheese, cumin, and garlic powder.

2. Spoon the mixture onto half of each tortilla, fold, and press to seal.

3. Air fry at 375°F (190°C) for 6-8 minutes until golden.
Serving: Serve with salsa or guacamole.
Cooking Time: 8 minutes

10. Jicama and Mango Salad Cups

Ingredients:
1. 1 medium jicama, peeled and julienned
2. 1 ripe mango, diced
3. 1/2 cup chopped red bell pepper
4. 1/4 cup chopped fresh cilantro
5. Juice of 2 limes
6. Tajin seasoning for garnish

Instructions:
1. In a bowl, combine jicama, mango, red bell pepper, cilantro, and lime juice.
2. Spoon the salad into individual serving cups.
3. Air fry at 375°F (190°C) for 5-7 minutes until the jicama softens slightly.
Serving: Sprinkle with Tajin seasoning before serving.
Cooking Time: 7 minutes

Chapter 3: Mexican Air Fryer Main Dishes Recipes

Here are 10 delicious Mexican Air Fryer main dish recipes for you:

1. Crispy Chicken Tacos with Avocado Lime Crema

Ingredients:
1. 1 pound boneless, skinless chicken thighs
2. 1 tablespoon taco seasoning
3. 1 cup breadcrumbs
4. 1 teaspoon cumin
5. 1 teaspoon paprika
6. Salt and pepper to taste
7. 8 small corn or flour tortillas
8. Shredded lettuce, diced tomatoes, and shredded cheese for toppings

Instructions:

1. Coat chicken thighs with taco seasoning, cumin, paprika, salt, and pepper.

2. Dredge in breadcrumbs, ensuring an even coating.

3. Air fry at 375°F (190°C) for 12-15 minutes until golden and cooked through.

4. Serve in tortillas with your favorite toppings and a drizzle of avocado lime crema.

Cooking Time: 15 minutes

2. Air Fried Beef Tostadas

Ingredients:

1. 1 pound ground beef
2. 1 packet taco seasoning
3. 8 tostada shells
4. 1 cup refried beans
5. Shredded lettuce, diced tomatoes, and guacamole for toppings
6. Shredded cheddar cheese for melting

Instructions:

1. Cook ground beef with taco seasoning until fully browned.
2. Spread refried beans on tostada shells.
3. Top with seasoned beef, cheese, and other desired toppings.
4. Air fry at 375°F (190°C) for 5-7 minutes until the cheese is melted.
Cooking Time: 7 minutes

3. Air Fryer Shrimp Tacos

Ingredients:
1. 1 pound of large shrimp, peeled and deveined
2. 1 tablespoon olive oil
3. 1 teaspoon chili powder
4. 1 teaspoon cumin
5. 1/2 teaspoon garlic powder
6. 8 small flour tortillas
7. Shredded cabbage, pico de gallo, and lime wedges for toppings
Instructions:
1. Toss shrimp with olive oil, chili powder, cumin, and garlic powder.

2. Air fry at 375°F (190°C) for 5-7 minutes until shrimp are opaque and cooked through.

3. Serve in tortillas with shredded cabbage, pico de gallo, and a squeeze of lime.

Cooking Time: 7 minutes

4. Crispy Carnitas Burrito Bowls

Ingredients:

1. 1 pound pork shoulder, diced into small cubes
2. 1 tablespoon olive oil
3. 1 teaspoon cumin
4. 1 teaspoon smoked paprika
5. 1 teaspoon oregano
6. Salt and pepper to taste
7. Cooked rice
8. Black beans, corn, diced tomatoes, and avocado for toppings

Instructions:

1. Toss pork cubes with olive oil, cumin, smoked paprika, oregano, salt, and pepper.

2. Air fry at 375°F (190°C) for 15-20 minutes until pork is crispy.

3. Serve over cooked rice with black beans, corn, diced tomatoes, and avocado.

Cooking Time: 20 minutes

5. Air Fried Fish Tacos with Cilantro Lime Slaw

Ingredients:

1. 1 pound white fish filets (tilapia or cod)

2. 1 cup breadcrumbs

3. 1 teaspoon chili powder

4. 1 teaspoon cumin

5. Salt and pepper to taste

6. 8 small corn tortillas

7. Shredded cabbage, cilantro lime slaw, and sliced radishes for toppings

Instructions:

1. Mix breadcrumbs with chili powder, cumin, salt, and pepper.

2. Dredge fish filets in breadcrumb mixture.

3. Air fry at 375°F (190°C) for 10-12 minutes until the fish is cooked and crispy.

4. Serve in tortillas with shredded cabbage, cilantro lime slaw, and sliced radishes.

Cooking Time: 12 minutes

6. Air Fryer Chicken Fajitas

Ingredients:

1. 1 pound chicken breasts, thinly sliced
2. 1 bell pepper, sliced
3. 1 onion, sliced
4. 1 tablespoon fajita seasoning
5. 2 tablespoons olive oil
6. Flour tortillas
7. Guacamole, sour cream, and salsa for toppings

Instructions:

1. Toss chicken, bell pepper, and onion with fajita seasoning and olive oil.

2. Air fry at 375°F (190°C) for 12-15 minutes until chicken is cooked and veggies are tender.

3. Serve in tortillas with guacamole, sour cream, and salsa.

Cooking Time: 15 minutes

7. Chile Relleno Casserole

Ingredients:

1. 4 poblano peppers, roasted and peeled
2. 1 cup shredded cheese (Monterey Jack or Oaxaca)
3. 1 cup cooked and shredded chicken
4. 4 large eggs
5. 1 cup milk
6. 1/2 cup all-purpose flour
7. 1 teaspoon baking powder
8. Salt and pepper to taste

Instructions:

1. Cut roasted and peeled poblano peppers into strips.
2. Layer peppers, shredded chicken, and cheese in an air fryer-safe dish.
3. In a bowl, whisk together eggs, milk, flour, baking powder, salt, and pepper.
4. Pour the egg mixture over the layered ingredients.

5. Air fry at 350°F (175°C) for 20-25 minutes until set.
Cooking Time: 25 minutes

8. Barbacoa Quesadillas

Ingredients:
1. 1 pound beef chuck roast, shredded
2. 1 cup beef broth
3. 1 tablespoon ground cumin
4. 1 tablespoon chili powder
5. 1 teaspoon dried oregano
6. 8 small flour tortillas
7. Shredded Monterey Jack cheese
8. Sliced pickled jalapeños for toppings

Instructions:
1. In a bowl, mix shredded beef, beef broth, cumin, chili powder, and oregano.
2. Place a portion of the beef mixture and cheese on half of each tortilla.
3. Fold tortillas in half and air fry at 375°F (190°C) for 6-8 minutes until crispy.
4. Top with sliced pickled jalapeños before serving.
Cooking Time: 8 minutes

9. Air Fried Chicken Enchiladas

Ingredients:
1. 1 pound cooked and shredded chicken
2. 1 cup black beans, drained and rinsed
3. 1 cup corn kernels
4. 1 teaspoon ground cumin
5. 1 teaspoon chili powder
6. 8 small corn tortillas
7. Enchilada sauce
8. Shredded cheddar cheese

Instructions:
1. In a bowl, mix shredded chicken, black beans, corn, cumin, and chili powder.
2. Spoon a portion of the mixture onto each tortilla, roll them up, and place seam-side down in the air fryer.
3. Pour enchilada sauce over the rolled tortillas and top with shredded cheddar cheese.
4. Air fry at 375°F (190°C) for 12-15 minutes until the cheese is melted and bubbly.

Cooking Time: 15 minutes

10. Air Fryer Beef Tamales

Ingredients:

1. 10 prepared beef tamales
2. 1 cup red enchilada sauce
3. 1 cup shredded Mexican cheese blend
4. Chopped fresh cilantro for garnish

Instructions:

1. Arrange tamales in the air fryer basket.
2. Pour enchilada sauce over the tamales and sprinkle with shredded cheese.
3. Air fry at 375°F (190°C) for 10-12 minutes until the cheese is melted and bubbly.
4. Garnish with chopped cilantro before serving.

Cooking Time: 12 minutes

Chapter 4: Mexican Air Fryer Dessert Recipes

1. Churro Bites with Chocolate Dipping Sauce

Ingredients:
1. 1 package refrigerated crescent roll dough
2. 1/4 cup sugar
3. 1 teaspoon ground cinnamon
4. Cooking spray
5. 1/2 cup chocolate chips
6. 2 tablespoons heavy cream

Instructions:
1. Unroll the crescent roll dough and cut it into bite-sized pieces.
2. Mix sugar and cinnamon in a bowl and coat each dough piece.
3. Place the coated dough pieces in the air fryer basket, spray with cooking spray, and air fry at 375°F (190°C) for 5-7 minutes until golden.

4. In a small saucepan, heat chocolate chips and heavy cream until smooth. Serve as a dipping sauce.

Cooking Time: 7 minutes

2. Sopapilla Cheesecake

Ingredients:

1. 2 cans refrigerated crescent roll dough
2. 16 ounces cream cheese, softened
3. 1 cup sugar
4. 1 teaspoon vanilla extract
5. 1/4 cup melted butter
6. 1 teaspoon ground cinnamon

Instructions:

1. The air fryer should be preheated to 350°F (175°C).
2. Roll out one can of crescent roll dough and press it into the bottom of an air fryer-safe pan.
3. In a small bowl, mix cream cheese, sugar, and vanilla. Spread over the crescent roll dough.
4. Roll out the second can of crescent roll dough and place it on top.

5. Pour melted butter over the top and sprinkle with cinnamon.

6. Air fry for 20-25 minutes until the top is golden and the center is set.

Cooking Time: 25 minutes

3. Mexican Chocolate Lava Cake

Ingredients:

1. 1/2 cup unsalted butter
2. 4 ounces Mexican chocolate, chopped
3. 1/2 cup powdered sugar
4. 2 large eggs
5. 2 egg yolks
6. 1/4 cup all-purpose flour
7. 1/2 teaspoon ground cinnamon
8. Pinch of cayenne pepper (optional)

Instructions:

1. In a microwave-safe bowl, melt the butter and Mexican chocolate together. Let it cool slightly.

2. Stir in powdered sugar, eggs, egg yolks, flour, cinnamon, and cayenne pepper.

3. Divide the batter into ramekins and place them in the air fryer basket.

4. Air fry at 375°F (190°C) for 10-12 minutes until the edges are set but the center is still soft.

Cooking Time: 12 minutes

4. Tres Leches Bread Pudding

Ingredients:

1. 4 cups cubed stale bread
2. 1 can evaporated milk
3. 1 can sweetened condensed milk
4. 1 cup whole milk
5. 4 large eggs
6. 1 teaspoon vanilla extract
7. 1/2 cup raisins (optional)
8. Ground cinnamon for dusting

Instructions:

1. In a bowl, mix evaporated milk, sweetened condensed milk, whole milk, eggs, and vanilla.
2. Place the cubed bread in the air fryer basket and pour the milk mixture over it.
3. Let it soak for 15 minutes, then sprinkle raisins on top.

4. Air fry at 350°F (175°C) for 20-25 minutes until the top is golden.

5. Dust with ground cinnamon before serving.

Cooking Time: 25 minutes

5. Pineapple Empanadas

Ingredients:

1. 1 cup canned crushed pineapple, drained

2. 1/4 cup brown sugar

3. 1 teaspoon ground cinnamon

4. 1 package refrigerated pie crusts

5. 1 egg, beaten

6. Powdered sugar for dusting

Instructions:

1. In a bowl, mix crushed pineapple, brown sugar, and cinnamon.

2. Roll out the pie crusts and cut them into circles.

3. Place a spoonful of pineapple mixture in the center of each circle.

4. Fold the circles in half, sealing the edges with a fork.

5. Brush the empanadas with beaten egg and air fry at 375°F (190°C) for 10-12 minutes until golden.

6. Dust with powdered sugar before serving.

Cooking Time: 12 minutes

6. Cajeta Stuffed Churro Twists

Ingredients:

1. 1 package refrigerated crescent roll dough

2. 1/2 cup cajeta (Mexican caramel sauce)

3. 1/4 cup sugar

4. 1 teaspoon ground cinnamon

5. Cooking spray

Instructions:

1. Unroll the crescent roll dough and separate it into triangles.

2. Spread a small amount of cajeta on each triangle and roll it up.

3. Mix sugar and cinnamon in a bowl, then coat each churro twist.

4. Place in the air fryer basket, spray with cooking spray, and air fry at 375°F (190°C) for 6-8 minutes until golden.
Cooking Time: 8 minutes

7. Mexican Flan Cups

Ingredients:
1. 1 cup sugar
2. 4 large eggs
3. 1 can sweetened condensed milk
4. 1 can evaporated milk
5. 1 teaspoon vanilla extract

Instructions:
1. In a saucepan, melt sugar over medium heat until golden brown.
2. Pour melted sugar into the bottom of individual oven-safe cups.
3. In a blender, mix eggs, sweetened condensed milk, evaporated milk, and vanilla until smooth.
4. Pour the mixture into the cups and place them in the air fryer basket.
5. Air fry at 350°F (175°C) for 15-20 minutes until the flan is set.

Cooking Time: 20 minutes

8. Mexican Hot Chocolate Cookies

Ingredients:
1. 1 cup unsalted butter, softened
2. 1 cup sugar
3. 2 large eggs
4. 1 teaspoon vanilla extract
5. 2 cups all-purpose flour
6. 1/2 cup cocoa powder
7. 1 teaspoon ground cinnamon
8. 1/2 teaspoon cayenne pepper
9. Powdered sugar for rolling

Instructions:
1. In a bowl, cream together butter and sugar. Add eggs and vanilla, mix well.
2. In a separate bowl, whisk together flour, cocoa powder, cinnamon, and cayenne pepper.
3. Gradually put the dry ingredients to the wet ingredients and mix until combined.
4. Roll the dough into balls, then roll each ball in powdered sugar.

5. Place the cookies in the air fryer basket and air fry at 350°F (175°C) for 8-10 minutes.

Cooking Time: 10 minutes

9. Dulce de Leche Banana Empanadas

Ingredients:

1. 2 ripe bananas, mashed
2. 1/2 cup dulce de leche
3. 1 package refrigerated pie crusts
4. 1 egg, beaten
5. Cinnamon sugar for dusting

Instructions:

1. Mix mashed bananas with dulce de leche.
2. Roll out the pie crusts and cut them into circles.
3. Place a spoonful of banana mixture in the center of each circle.
4. Fold the circles in half, sealing the edges with a fork.
5. Brush the empanadas with beaten egg, sprinkle with cinnamon sugar, and air fry at 375°F (190°C) for 10-12 minutes.

Cooking Time: 12 minutes

10. Mango Coconut Rice Pudding

Ingredients:
1. 1 cup cooked rice
2. 1 cup coconut milk
3. 1/2 cup mango puree
4. 1/4 cup sugar
5. 1/2 teaspoon vanilla extract

Instructions:
1. In a saucepan, combine cooked rice, coconut milk, mango puree, sugar, and vanilla.
2. Cook on low heat until the mixture thickens.
3. Transfer the rice pudding into individual serving bowls and let it cool.
4. Place the bowls in the air fryer basket and air fry at 350°F (175°C) for 5-7 minutes until the top is lightly browned.

Cooking Time: 7 minutes

Chapter 5: Mexican Air Fryer Quick Fries Recipes

Here are 5 quick and delicious Mexican Air Fryer fries recipes for you:

1. Crispy Chili Lime Sweet Potato Fries

Ingredients:
1. 2 large sweet potatoes, cut into fries
2. 2 tablespoons olive oil
3. 1 teaspoon chili powder
4. 1 teaspoon ground cumin
5. Zest and juice of 1 lime
6. Salt and pepper to taste

Instructions:
1. Toss sweet potato fries with olive oil, chili powder, cumin, lime zest, lime juice, salt, and pepper.
2. Place the fries in the air fryer basket and air fry at 400°F (200°C) for 15-20 minutes until crispy and golden.

Cooking Time: 20 minutes

2. Mexican Street Corn Fries

Ingredients:
1. 2 large russet potatoes, cut into fries
2. 2 tablespoons olive oil
3. 1 teaspoon chili powder
4. 1/2 cup crumbled cotija cheese
5. 1/4 cup chopped fresh cilantro
6. Lime wedges for serving

Instructions:
1. Toss potato fries with olive oil and chili powder.
2. Air fry at 400°F (200°C) for 18-20 minutes until fries are crispy.
3. Sprinkle cotija cheese and cilantro over the fries.
4. Serve with lime slices on the side.

Cooking Time: 20 minutes

3. Spicy Guacamole Fries

Ingredients:
1. 2 large russet potatoes, cut into fries
2. 2 tablespoons olive oil
3. 1 teaspoon cayenne pepper
4. 1/2 cup guacamole
5. 1/4 cup diced tomatoes
6. 2 tablespoons chopped green onions

Instructions:
1. Toss potato fries with olive oil and cayenne pepper.
2. Air fry at 400°F (200°C) for 18-20 minutes until fries are golden and crispy.
3. Spread guacamole over the fries and top with diced tomatoes and green onions.

Cooking Time: 20 minutes

4. Queso Fundido Loaded Fries

Ingredients:
1. 2 large russet potatoes, cut into fries
2. 2 tablespoons olive oil

3. 1 cup shredded Oaxaca or Monterey Jack cheese

4. 1/2 cup cooked chorizo

5. 1/4 cup chopped fresh cilantro

Instructions:

1. Toss potato fries with olive oil.

2. Air fry at 400°F (200°C) for 18-20 minutes until fries are crispy.

3. Top with shredded cheese and cooked chorizo.

4. Air fry for an additional 3-5 minutes until the cheese is melted.

5. Garnish with fresh cilantro before serving.

Cooking Time: 20 minutes

5. Adobo Seasoned Crispy Fries

Ingredients:

1. 2 large russet potatoes, cut into fries

2. 2 tablespoons olive oil

3. 1 teaspoon adobo seasoning

4. 1/2 teaspoon garlic powder

5. 1/2 teaspoon onion powder

6. 1/4 cup chopped fresh parsley

Instructions:

1. Toss potato fries with olive oil, adobo seasoning, garlic powder, and onion powder.

2. Air fry at 400°F (200°C) for 18-20 minutes until fries are golden and crispy.

3. Sprinkle chopped parsley over the fries before serving.

Cooking Time: 20 minutes

6. Jalapeño Popper Loaded Fries

Ingredients:

1. 2 large russet potatoes, cut into fries

2. 2 tablespoons olive oil

3. 1 cup shredded cheddar cheese

4. 1/2 cup cream cheese, softened

5. 2 jalapeños, sliced (seeds removed for less heat)

6. 4 slices cooked and crumbled bacon

7. Chopped green onions for garnish

Instructions:

1. Toss potato fries with olive oil.

2. Air fry at 400°F (200°C) for 18-20 minutes until fries are crispy.

3. Mix shredded cheddar and softened cream cheese, spread over the fries.

4. Top with jalapeño slices and bacon.

5. Air fry for an additional 3-5 minutes until the cheese is melted.

6. Garnish with chopped or slices green onions before serving.

Cooking Time: 20 minutes

7. Tajin Lime Zucchini Fries

Ingredients:

1. 2 large zucchinis, cut into fries
2. 2 tablespoons olive oil
3. 2 teaspoons Tajin seasoning
4. Zest and juice of 1 lime
5. Salt to taste

Instructions:

1. Toss zucchini fries with olive oil, Tajin seasoning, lime zest, lime juice, and salt.

2. Air fry at 400°F (200°C) for 12-15 minutes until fries are golden and crispy.

Cooking Time: 15 minutes

8. Mole-Inspired Sweet Potato Fries

Ingredients:
1. 2 large sweet potatoes, cut into fries
2. 2 tablespoons olive oil
3. 2 teaspoons mole sauce
4. 1 teaspoon ground cinnamon
5. Salt to taste

Instructions:
1. Toss sweet potato fries with olive oil, mole sauce, ground cinnamon, and salt.
2. Air fry at 400°F (200°C) for 15-18 minutes until fries are crispy and caramelized.

Cooking Time: 18 minutes

9. Chili Garlic Avocado Fries

Ingredients:
1. 2 large avocados, sliced into fries
2. 1/2 cup flour
3. 2 eggs, beaten
4. 1 cup panko breadcrumbs
5. 1 teaspoon chili garlic sauce
6. Lime wedges for serving

Instructions:

1. Dredge avocado slices in flour, dip in beaten eggs, and coat with panko breadcrumbs.

2. Place in the air fryer basket and air fry at 400°F (200°C) for 8-10 minutes until golden.

3. Mix chili garlic sauce and drizzle over the avocado fries.

4. Serve with lime slices on the side.

Cooking Time: 10 minutes

10. Chipotle Ranch Potato Wedges

Ingredients:

1. 4 large russet potatoes, cut into wedges

2. 2 tablespoons olive oil

3. 1 teaspoon chipotle powder

4. 1 teaspoon garlic powder

5. 1/2 cup ranch dressing for dipping

Instructions:

1. Toss potato wedges with olive oil, chipotle powder, and garlic powder.

2. Air fry at 400°F (200°C) for 20-25 minutes until wedges are crispy.

3. Serve with a side of ranch dressing for dipping.
Cooking Time: 25 minutes

Conclusion

As we bid you farewell on this culinary journey, may your kitchen forever echo with the vibrant flavors and aromas of Mexico. Through the sizzling sounds of the air fryer, you've embarked on a quest to marry the rich traditions of Mexican cuisine with the modern convenience of air frying. From crispy appetizers to succulent main dishes and indulgent desserts, each recipe has been crafted to transport you to the heart of Mexico, celebrating the warmth of its people and the zestiness of its culinary heritage.

As you embark on your own cooking adventures, remember the joy that great food brings — the laughter shared around a table, the stories exchanged, and the bonds strengthened. May these recipes become a delightful addition to your kitchen repertoire, infusing it with the spirit of Mexico and the thrill of discovering new flavors.

So, with a sprinkle of cilantro, a squeeze of lime, and a dash of Mexican flair, we invite you to embrace the art of air frying with these tantalizing recipes. ¡Hasta la próxima! Until we meet again in the kitchen, may your culinary endeavors be filled with love, flavor, and the everlasting spirit of Mexican gastronomy.

¡Buen provecho y que viva la buena comida! (Enjoy your meal and long live good food!)

Printed in Great Britain
by Amazon